Re-v
Confirmation for Mission and Discipleship

Charles Chadwick
Parish Development Adviser, Diocese of Oxford

Phillip Tovey
Warden of Readers Emeritus
Retired Principal of Oxford LMP

GROVE BOOKS LIMITED
RIDLEY HALL RD CAMBRIDGE CB3 9HU

Contents

Acknowledgments

We want to thank all those who have been willing to share their story and insights with us.
We also thank Coryn Standforth for comments on the text.

First Impression February 2023
ISSN 0144-1728
ISBN 978 1 78827 293 3

1 Introduction

This book does not rehearse the theological debates on confirmation, or commend practices from the past. The authors have the conviction that baptism is complete and does not need finishing or topping up. Nevertheless, we think confirmation has three positive elements:

- *Pastoral*. It is a time to work with lay people exploring their Christian journey. This has often involved some teaching or discipleship development.
- *Missional*. Hearing about faith development can be inspirational. 'If they have taken this step, why not me?' The journey to confirmation can also equip people to say something about their faith.
- *Sacramental*. It is an opportunity to revisit and renew the commitments of baptism in the context of a prayer of blessing by a church leader and an invocation of the Spirit. It might be and has been the point where people are included as communicants in the church.

Confirmation is a pastoral and missional opportunity for the church and for the faith journey of the individual. It is a part of our discipleship of the Jesus who said, 'Follow me.'

In the following chapters we will look at some of the paths people follow. We will look at those baptized as infants and confirmed later in life. This is the classic approach found in the *Book of Common Prayer*. We will then look at those baptized and admitted to Communion before confirmation, an increasingly common approach in England and the approach in other Provinces (Wales, USA, New Zealand). The we will look at those who are baptized as adults and possibly confirmed at baptism. Finally, we will consider the place of teaching and formation in the process to confirmation.

We are convinced that story is important. The chapters will include stories we have gathered to give flesh to the statistics. Ultimately, we are dealing with real people and their journey in faith. For many, confirmation is an important step in their development. Bishops, also, will have views on what they are doing, so our first story is from a retired bishop.

The Bishop's Story

The last twenty years have seen changes in people's appreciation of confirmation. In an era which has concerns about the legitimacy and expression of institutions, it is unlikely that people will describe their confirmation as being to do with joining the institution, that is, the Church of England.

While to be confirmed is often to do with ownership of what has taken place when one is an infant, and is to do with one's identity, it should be acknowledged that one's sense of identity at aged 11, 13 and 17 is likely to be different.

In some dioceses, at least half of the young people being confirmed do so via their school. Over the last fifty years have seen a change from 'Everyone gets confirmed here' to an invitation to explore confirmation and to be confirmed because one wants to for oneself. The role of family is likely to be important with young people appreciating and acknowledging what their parents and godparent said on their behalf when they were baptized at a very young age.

Setting the Scene

2

For several years, we have been conducting an examination of the initiation statistics of the Diocese of Oxford. The diocese follows the national trend of a decline in numbers of baptisms and confirmations. Within those figures there are churches which still conduct large numbers of infant baptisms, and others with large numbers of adult baptisms. Confirmations are declining and it might be argued that the health of the present figures is propped up by the large number of school confirmations conducted. Phillip has also been writing more in-depth about the history of confirmation.[1] People's stories show variety in paths of growth.

Nicholas

I was baptized as an infant in London. As a schoolboy I read *Honest to God* by John Robinson and that led me to become an atheist. As I prepared to become a parent for the first time some 13 years later, I decided it was time to commit. I was confirmed in 1976 in my parish church in North London. Later I began attending a church in central London. We stayed there for 16 years until we left London. Early on I went on a retreat and since then I have made attending Communion, saying the daily office each morning, and saying prayers at bedtime each night, as the basis of my devotional life. For me, spiritual growth has been a slow and gradual process with it taking some time to move from my confirmation, then to regular church attendance and then to daily prayer. I believe my devotional life has helped me become a better person.

The meaning of confirmation has been much debated and changed in the last 100 years.[2] Some of the theologies put forward were a particular Victorian development with disastrous ecumenical implications.[3] Within the Anglican Communion there has been much debate, particularly centring around the idea of a baptismal covenant leading to Communion. This has questioned the traditional link between confirmation and Holy Communion (as can be seen in Margaret below); thus now many parishes admit people to Communion before confirmation. So, what is the point of being confirmed? Others have used the rite of passage theory to dismiss confirmation somewhat, but this is not the story of Nicholas above. The danger here is that, if confirmation is a teenage rite of passage, then what does it mean for adults? There is much confusion in ministers' minds, which does not lead to an easy commendation of confirmation. A lead by the bishops might help the situation.

Margaret

I was confirmed aged 14 on Advent Sunday in 1964 by the Bishop of Connor. The service was preceded by six months of regular preparation classes led by the rector, which did not feel too bad as I was attending them with my friends. On the day itself there was a great emphasis on the white dress and veil I and all the other girls had to wear, with the rector's wife checking there was nothing in our veils that might scratch the bishop's hand. The boys wore their school uniforms. The church was packed, with 30 of us being confirmed, and I much enjoyed it. My parents and godparents were there along with a very large congregation. The first time I received Holy Communion was the next Sunday at 8.30am as the church only had the Communion service once a month. I look back on my confirmation with appreciation and still remember the day every year.

In contrast to the previous centuries the numbers are now very low.[4] Confirmation included large numbers in the eighteenth-century and number grew for much of the nineteenth-century. After decline in the interwar period, confirmations grew again till the 1960s and then declined.

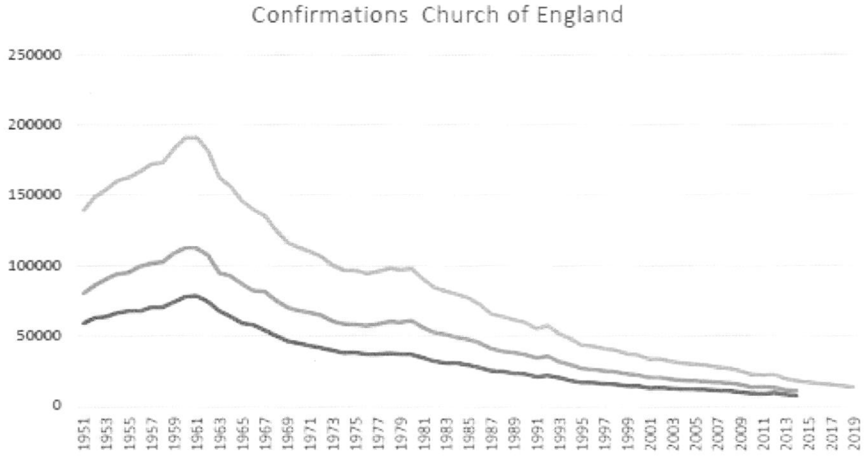

Confirmation Chart[5] Top line = male Middle line = female Bottom line = total

The rate of decline is constant and does not show any sign of slowing. There are a few upward blips, but these do not arrest the overall decline. Also, in the 1980s, 25% of those baptised got confirmed, now only 10% are confirmed. Confirmation has been seen as an indicator of adult commitment in the church.[6] We need to be aware that for many, confirmation is significant, as in Hannah's story, but the statistics are concerning.

Hannah

I was dedicated as a baby and baptized and confirmed at the same time when I was 15. Confirmation was raised as a possibility by our youth worker whom I knew well, and he chatted with me about my faith. About ten of us were baptized and confirmed at the same time which felt exciting. To have my parents and grandparents at the service was special too. I chose to be baptized outside the church in a pool as I felt the symbolism was important. For me to publicly say, 'This is who I am, and yes, I follow Jesus,' felt like a special time. That the church really celebrated the occasion added to it all.

Bishops still use the model developed by Samuel Wilberforce, of going to the people and doing as many confirmations as possible, even with very small numbers. The eighteenth-century bishop expected people to come to him, and the 2019 numbers would have possibly been done in one service in the eighteenth century!

Questions

- What is the story of your baptism and confirmation?
- What part did they take in your journey of faith?
- When did your church last do confirmations?

3 Confirmation After Infant Baptism

The first *Books of Common Prayer* were written for a society that was almost exclusively Christian with one church. There are no services of adult baptism because there were no adults to baptize. The whole society was presumed Christian and there was a simple model of infant baptism followed by catechism and confirmation, as Emma's story shows. This does not mean that there were tensions in the model, not least concerning the provision of bishops.

> **Emma**
> I was baptized when I was five months old and confirmed at the age of 12. It is hard to put into words exactly why I wanted to be confirmed, but I wanted to affirm what was already in place. It was good to do it with a friend and be part of a group of people of all ages, particularly to share insights and ideas with them. To be able to receive Holy Communion as a result of being confirmed helped me to feel more involved in the service. Now I am in my late twenties I like to attend church for the main festivals and to receive Holy Communion then.

Age of Discretion

One of the prevailing problems was the age of confirmation. The 1662 book talks of the 'years of discretion.' So no fixed age is given but a concept. Legally it is when the law looks on you as responsible for your actions. Another understanding is when you become an adult. Another is when you can 'understand' the sacraments. This latter idea possibly is connected to Paul's warnings in 1 Corinthians 11 about discerning the body. This then connects confirmation, at the age of discernment, to receiving Communion, a traditional understanding.

The debate about the age of confirmation continues. Today bishops will probably set out a minimum age. In history this has varied considerably. For a long time, the age was set at 7. At this point you were supposed to be able to have sufficient understanding to receive Communion. However, despite a suggested norm of 7, in 1553 Elizabeth I was baptized and confirmed at 3 days old.[7] Infant confirmation happened, even if it was a rare practice. For a lot of Anglican history, the age was set at 14/15. This was the age at which you became an adult and could work for a living (if not before). Changes in education, law and psychological development theory also contribute to the age of discernment question, making it more complex.

The Role of Institutions in Fostering Confirmation

The nineteenth century saw the introduction of confirmation to schools. This was in part due to the reforms of Mathew Arnold and the Tractarian movement. Schools and particularly boarding schools were places for a thorough Christian education and formation. There is no doubt that this has been significant for many who were educated in such a way. Geoff's story is of school confirmation, more in the 'everyone gets done' mode that is dying out.

> **Geoff**
>
> I was christened as an infant, but then brought up without any involvement in church. At my boarding school the chaplain wanted me to be confirmed at 15 but I excused myself. He insisted I should be confirmed the following year, which I duly did, but without much clue about it or any personal commitment to the faith. My faith began to stir through a friend at school and a significant conversation during my gap year. I went off to college looking for meaning and faith. There I met Christians with a personal relationship with God and I wanted what they had. I invited Jesus into my life in the study of an Anglican vicar who then invited me to meet with him twice a week to pray and read the Bible; but I had no liturgical markers for that part of my journey because they had taken place before I had made any profession of faith.

Today the boarding schools contribute a significant proportion of the candidates for confirmation. Their contained environment has been less permeable to outside forces than most parishes. Other institutions including prisons can provide a community in which people may respond to God, as this story shows.

> **From a Prison Chaplain**
>
> The impetus for offering confirmation in a prison came from a prisoner who mentioned to the chaplaincy team that it was a long-held wish of his grandmother that he be confirmed. On offering the possibility of confirmation across the prison, a number of prisoners, who were on the same wing as the prisoner who had first raised it, expressed an interest in also being confirmed. One might describe this as engagement with confirmation by contagion.
>
> Rather than having a series of classes or a set course, the chaplaincy team offered a series of four conversations, each of which lasted thirty

minutes. The classes covered the following areas: the Old Testament; Jesus and the gospels; stories from the Bible; and the confirmation service.

The chaplains discovered that for the prisoners the most strongly articulated aspect of the whole process was the act of being confirmed itself. This was more important to the prisoners than learning details of the Christian faith and life. It appears that to be confirmed, and to have a photograph with the officiating bishop, was a way of making an important statement about one's identity for oneself.

Drawing on the example of schools and prisons and given the involvement of many parishes in their local care and nursing homes, one might wonder about offering some form of faith exploration and discussions potentially leading to confirmation, specifically tailored to the people in that context. For bishops to be seen and experienced as confirming people of a mature age would be saying something significant about the church truly being intergenerational.

Confirmation and Communion

Many would argue that the model, 'you get confirmed and then receive Communion,' seems simple. In practice this did not work out so easily. It would appear the medieval church tried to keep this simple discipline, hence the final rubric 'None be admitted to the Holy Communion until…he be confirmed.' This was taken from the *Sarum Manual* which was itself based on Archbishop Peckham's Constitutions of 1281.[8] Usually such rules are introduced to counter a problem, which would suggest that many came to mass unconfirmed and may be confirmation was not regarded as significant as long as you could receive Communion a few times a year.

After the Reformation problems continued. Many were confirmed but far fewer received Communion either occasionally or at all. A consequence of the Reformation was that the usual pattern for Sunday worship was Morning and Evening Prayer, with the hearing and preaching of the Word being the main liturgical emphasis, and Communion only occurring monthly, as Margaret's story in chapter one reveals. While Canon B15 states that it is the duty of all who have been confirmed to receive the Holy Communion regularly, and especially at the festivals of Christmas, Easter and Whitsun or Pentecost, as with other aspects of church life, quite what 'regularly' meant remained open to wide interpretation. The gap between the confirmed and communicants was a major issue of discussion right up to the 1960s.[9] Not all who were baptized were confirmed, and even fewer became communicants. This is a structural problem in the church that has lasted for many years and is still an issue in some places.

Part of the issue may be that reticence and respect for Communion grew in response to the warnings in 1 Corinthians (1 Cor 11. 27–31). This also encouraged the need for proper and respectful preparation. Bishop Michael Ramsey, when Bishop of Durham, said, 'Holy Communion...is a responsible act of an individual and that is an act full of awe and dread.'[10] In the same address the bishop goes on, 'There is too often a lack of teaching, bringing in its train a lack of meaningfulness and reverent understanding. And this is seen especially in a misleading notion of offering and sacrifice, a disregard of the character of Communion as a responsible and dreadful act on the part of the individual, and an idea of fellowship which is less than Christian.'

In parts of Anglican history there was no bishop. In such times, people have been admitted to Communion by the priest.[11]

Repeatability

Anglican practice in the eighteenth century included those who were confirmed several times. Some people thought you could 'not get enough of a good thing,' and repeatedly went forward. The church tried to cut out this practice by improving the administration of the rite.

Max Thurian in the *Consecration of the Layman* argued for a repeatable 'consecration.' He looked at the apostle Paul who received his initiation in Damascus (Acts 9.17–19) but decided that this did not exclude further consecrations for missionary work (Acts 13.1–3). Thurian saw the need for further occasions for the laying on of hands, even suggesting an annual action. As one goes through life and different things happen the journey might be marked by a laying on of hands. This could be done by the rite of Affirmation of Faith but there might also need to be more of a commissioning element, as we will see later.

Conclusion

When and where people have both been confirmed and begun to receive Holy Communion has varied over time and this is likely to continue. Fostering a culture where the faith can be explored and discussed and inviting people to be part of it is important. Confirmation needs to be a natural expression of church life, developing faith and discipleship.

Questions

- At what age were you confirmed? What did it mean to you then? Now?
- Do you think confirmation is necessary before Communion? Why?
- How do other people's stories compare with yours?

4 Confirmation After Receiving Communion

There has been a long debate about the requirement of confirmation as a condition for admission to Holy Communion.[12] The story of George and Ewan is about being admitted to Communion before confirmation.

George and Ewan
George who is now aged 10 and his brother Ewan aged 6 are regulars at their parish church which is also attended by their parents and grandparents. They spoke of receiving Holy Communion as being a great experience and they feel closer to God. Also, it is what everyone else is doing. They feel proud to be communicant members of the church. Their mother spoke of it being good that all three generations in her family receive Holy Communion together in their church.

The rubric in the 1662 confirmation service makes it almost absolute. 'There shall be none admitted to the Holy Communion until such time as he be confirmed.' But there is a qualifier to this 'or be ready and desirous to be confirmed.' The latter was used to admit people to Communion, if they were baptized as an adult when confirmation was only on the rare episcopal visit or where there were no Anglican bishops, *eg* the Channel Islands in World War 2.

Debating the Place of Confirmation

A new discussion arose in Anglicanism in the 1970s about the place of confirmation and Communion. In England it became visible with the Ely Report *Christian Initiation: Birth and Growth in the Christian Society* (1977) which stated:

> It should be permissible to admit baptized Christians to Communion after preparation without using Confirmation as some kind of spiritual or educational qualification.[13]

The Episcopal Church in the United States earlier accepted this position. Authorized Services (1973) said, 'Baptized persons in good standing are eligible to receive Holy Communion,'[14] and 'Holy baptism is full initiation by water and the Holy Spirit.'[15] These views were fundamental to the 1979 US *Book of Common Prayer*.

In England there was a seesaw debate over many years but gradually parishes were allowed to admit people before confirmation. The report *Rooted in the Church* recommends:

> The majority of our parent and young adult respondents indicated that they believed the linking of Communion to confirmation creates an artificial divide between generations in the church.[16]

And

> Churches should be encouraged to consider the possibility of admitting baptized children to Communion before confirmation.[17]

Most dioceses have a policy document about following this path.[18] The present regulations are from 2006 and enshrined in Canon B15A (c).[19] The debate has led to a service of Admission of the Baptized to Communion, and a sequence of baptism-admission-confirmation all with suitable catechesis.[20] Mary's story indicates there are different approaches in other denominations and thus ecumenical dimensions:

Mary

My family were Roman Catholics, and I was baptized at just a few weeks old in our Roman Catholic church, English Martyrs. We went to mass weekly and at the age of seven I received instruction on how to receive the sacrament including how to allow the priest to place the wafer on my tongue and not to chew the wafer. I made my first Communion wearing a white dress and veil which my mother made.

In my early twenties I met the man who is now my husband, and he was a regular attender at his Anglican parish church in which we were married. After our wedding, I would go to church with him and receive Holy Communion, which I still do. I have never felt the need to be confirmed.

The Church in Wales start from the point of all baptized children be admitted to Communion.[21] But if you are communicant, why be confirmed as Mary's story above indicates?

Confirmation After Communion?

For some people the idea of having confirmation after being a communicant is difficult to accept. They may have been receiving Communion for as long as they can remember; what more is needed? Each week at the Eucharistic

Prayer there is an epiclesis (calling down) of the Spirit on the people, so why do you need another occasion to invoke the Spirit?

The Ely Report assumed the situation of people receiving Communion before confirmation. It recommended that the rite of confirmation be a service of commitment and commissioning. This has never really happened. There are elements of commitment in *Common Worship: Holy Baptism* in the alternative Commission.

> Will you continue in the apostles' teaching and fellowship, in the breaking of bread, and in the prayers?
> **With the help of God, I will.**
>
> Will you persevere in resisting evil, and, whenever you fall into sin, repent and return to the Lord?
> **With the help of God, I will.**
>
> Will you proclaim by word and example the good news of God in Christ?
> **With the help of God, I will.**
>
> Will you seek and serve Christ in all people, loving your neighbour as yourself?
> **With the help of God, I will.**
>
> Will you acknowledge Christ's authority over human society, by prayer for the world and its leaders, by defending the weak, and by seeking peace and justice?
> **With the help of God, I will.**
>
> Will you strive to safeguard the integrity of creation, and sustain and renew the life of the earth?
> **With the help of God, I will.**
>
> May Christ dwell in your heart(s) through faith, that you may be rooted and grounded in love and bring forth the fruit of the Spirit.
> Amen.[22]

The last question was added by the Bishop of Oxford in his diocese to highlight climate concerns. However, this is not quite the commitment ceremony that some had envisaged and so later the chapter will look at the approach of other Provinces.[23] There is also a question about the language of this section; could there be an alternative in plainer English?

The Affirmation of Christian Faith service might be useful for further commitment, but it is more for those who have lapsed.[24] A regular communicant can hardly be called lapsed. The new year service in *Times and Seasons* include a personal commission based on the Methodist Covenant Service.[25] This is perhaps the most appropriate Common Worship material, we could learn from other Provinces.

Kenya

Our Modern Services (2002) envisaged the admission of those baptized in infancy to Communion at the age of 9–10. A separate service was included for this. After 12 they can go to a different service which is called 'Confirmation and Commissioning.' This is ordered as below.[26]

Call to Worship
Presentation
Ministry of the Word
Making of Promises
Confirmation
Commissioning
Peace
Communion

The Making of Promises is similar to the commission above but perhaps a bit more direct:

Will you be willing to tell your neighbours about the love of Christ?
I will.

Will you pray and support your church, the bishops, clergy and all the other church workers?
I will do so, God being my helper.

Will you read the Bible regularly and fashion your life after it?
I will diligently do so.

Will you endeavour to meet with other Christians for fellowship and stir up the gift of God that is in you?
I will endeavour to do so.

Will you make every effort to attend Sunday worship and in particular the celebration of Holy Communion?
I will do so.

Will you pursue justice, truth and reconciliation of God's people?
I will do so whenever opportunities arise.

Will you endeavour to feed the hungry, give water to the thirsty, welcome the needy, clothe the naked, visit the sick and those in prison?
I will do so with the help of God.

Will you support and pray for the lonely, the orphans, widows and all the voiceless?
I will support and pray for them.

Will you endeavour to be a good steward of God's creation and care for the environment?
I will endeavour to do so.

Will you be a faithful citizen of your nation, and regularly pray for its leaders?
I will.
Will you be alert and watchful, and firmly resist your enemy the devil?
I will do so with the help of God.

The alternative to this is a pledge by the candidate:

I, about to be commissioned for service and witness to Christ and his church, pledge to keep and walk in God's commandments all the days of my life, and to read the Bible and pray regularly. I pledge to proclaim Christ in season and out of season, to obey him and to live in the fellowship of all true believers throughout the world. I pledge to be active in the church, to give to the work of the church, to help the needy, support the poor, and to be a good steward of all that the Lord gives me. I pledge to uphold truth and justice, and to seek reconciliation among all people; Christ being my helper.

The brief confirmation prayer makes clear it is a prayer for one who already has the Spirit:

Strengthen, O Lord, your servant N with your Holy Spirit. Empower *him* for your service and sustain *him* all the days of his life. **Amen.**

A similar approach has been taken in New Zealand Aotearoa.[27] These are perhaps the type of services that the Ely Report envisaged.

Rites of Commitment and Blessing

As the number of people who have receive Communion at an early age increases, the Church of England may need to think more about a rite of commitment. But there are other possibilities of blessing; Max Thurian envisaged a repeatable 'confirmation' for stages in life and major life events (moving, new job, retiring). Modern confirmation debate extends the pastoral and missional opportunities, rather than closing them down. Perhaps gate-holders need to ask for a vision of what might be.

Questions

- If people are already communicants, why might they want to be confirmed?
- In the light of their commissioning, how might the confirmed create a rule of life?
- How do members of your church see confirmation?

5 Confirmation After Adult Baptism

The Church of England conducted 9,170 adult baptisms in 2019, 11% of the total number of baptisms.[28] In the same year 2,000 adults were confirmed, 45% of the total.[29] This somewhat undermines the view that confirmation is principally an adolescent rite of passage as almost half of the candidates were adults, as Sarah's story shows. The situation has radically transformed from the time where one could talk of indiscriminate confirmation.[30]

Sarah's Story

Sarah had left school and was beginning to become a hairdresser, working on qualifications at her local college and also in work at a local salon. One of the girls at the salon invited her to her wedding and she became fascinated by the church. She began to help with children's church on Sundays and gradually came to faith. Not having been baptized she began classes with the vicar and joined a large celebration at the cathedral for baptism and confirmation on Easter Day. She was glad that a friend from the group was also getting baptized, but it was one of the happier days of her life. The service was also her first time in receiving Communion. Cake was served in her local church after the service the next Sunday in honour of those baptized and confirmed.

The report *Baptism and Confirmation* (1958) recognized that 'in the New Testament adult baptism is the norm.'[31] It then worked from adult baptism to infant baptism in understanding the sacrament. Liturgically it arranged baptism and confirmation of adults as the archetype service, from which other services are derived (baptism of infants, confirmation). The report also emphasized the link between baptism, confirmation and Holy Communion, putting them all together in one service. This was the way that the *Alternative Service Book* was arranged, and it is the approach of *Common Worship*.

Our study of the parishes in the Diocese of Oxford showed that some churches regularly have adult baptisms, but that many have only a few, and a worrying number of parishes have no adult baptisms at all and have not done so for decades. Today it is false to make an assumption that any group we encounter is made up of baptized people, as Tim's story shows. Indeed, one of our incumbents said that he makes the assumption that most people he encounters are not baptized and need to hear the good news. Baptism (and confirmation) are a part of the mission of the church. It is unfortunate that some of the more popular catechetical schemes, like *Alpha*, do not make this connection.

> **Tim's Story**
>
> I grew up in a family with very little connection to anything religious. We might occasionally go to a Christmas carol service, but this was usually at school. Dad died just before I went to university and the chaplain at the hospice was very helpful. She led the family funeral at the crem.
>
> At uni I met some Christians for the first time, and they included me in their group. I began to ask questions about God and Jesus, and I began to think about faith. In the holidays I managed to go to a midweek service in my lunchtime at home.
>
> I got married to a girl in the Christian group and when we set up home, we wanted a church wedding. Noticing that I was not baptized, the vicar suggested baptism before the wedding (a year ahead). We did some classes, which were fun, and I was baptized in a large pool in the church six months before the wedding.
>
> I heard about confirmation but wanted to do our wedding first. I see it as a step into the mission of the church through my work and family.

In Tim's story the baptism and later confirmation are picked up through a pastoral connection, namely his wedding. The Spirit had been working through previous encounters and now in Tim's new life he wanted to follow the Christian way. The brief encounter of the meeting for booking the wedding opened the possibility of Tim professing his faith in baptism, a key step in discipleship. The journey continued in marriage, confirmation and everyday faith. We believe that for clergy to be alert to the potential of the pastoral offices to offer occasions when people may raise larger questions about their life and its meaning, has merit in terms of pastoral care for people at a time of transition and is missional in that such times may lead to people being open to the message of Christ.

Canon B24 on adult baptism requires the minister to instruct the candidate, inform the bishop, and get the candidate confirmed as soon as possible. This of course is possible if the archetypical service is used with the bishop present. The bishop then needs to preside over the whole service to avoid the idea that confirmation is the more important bit of the service. John Sentamu baptizing adults in a pool outside York Minster on Easter Day is a good example of practice. He was not afraid to get wet, use it as a public witness and missional drama![32]

What if the bishop is not available? The canon envisages a separate confirmation as soon as possible after the baptism. In these circumstances it becomes more difficult to give a rationale for confirmation. Why repeat the promises of baptism when you did that as an adult a few weeks before? Episcopal confirmation is not absolute in the Anglican Communion or in other sister churches (such as the Lutherans). There might be a case for the delegation of confirmation to presbyters in the absence of a bishop.[33] Delegation of confirmation to a presbyter is also allowed in the Roman Catholic Church under canon 884.[34]

A different situation arises with those baptized as adults in a church which follows the anabaptist tradition and rejects infant baptism. Considerable convergence in theology and practice has been the fruit of Anglican–Baptist dialogue and the report *Conversations Around the World* (2005) deserves being better known.[35] One way of responding to such people joining Anglican congregations is to simply welcome them to the table. The only restriction in the Church of England to a Baptist who has become a regular worshipper in a congregation is that the Church Representation Rules require a layperson to be confirmed to join General Synod (50.3.A). Many might not consider that a problem.

Jim and Wendy's Story

Jim and Wendy had both grown up in Baptist churches and were baptized as teenagers by full immersion. On retirement, the church they felt most comfortable in was the daughter church in a parish. They became regular communicants but could see no need for confirmation. They had both been at churches where the laying on of hands with prayer was a part of the baptismal service. Why did they need a bishop? was their question.

Hard lines of denominational identity have been eroded and this is to be welcomed. In the past Jim and Wendy would have been pressured to be confirmed as a change of denominational identity. While this is a possibility, they only need to be confirmed if they want to become Readers, get ordained or stand for election to General Synod.

However, that does not mean that there are no pastoral and liturgical opportunities. If a local church is keeping an eye on people transferring from other denominations then they might want to run a regular service of *Affirmation of Baptismal Faith*; this includes prayers for the candidates, a renewal of baptismal vows and a hand laying (but not necessarily by a bishop).[36] It is not the *Welcome into the Church of England* (for those baptized and confirmed now becoming Anglicans, for example, Roman Catholics and Orthodox), but it is a chance to recognize a transfer publicly.[37] There is also a catechetical opportunity to explain to those transferring about the Church of England. Many who join from other denominations find the Church of England somewhat baffling!

Chun Wai

Chun Wai had migrated from Hong Kong. Wandering into a church one Sunday, he found a friendly atmosphere and good chat after coffee. After a few weeks he plucked up courage to ask the minister a question: 'What is the Bible?' Over some weeks further discussion took place, and Chun Wai joined an *Emmaus* Group. The friendly people were Christians, and they talked a lot about Jesus. Coming to faith, Chun Wai was baptized by full immersion in the tank the church had built in the sanctuary and then, as it was an ecumenical church, confirmed by the bishop and a Methodist minister, and welcomed into the Baptist Church.

Chun Wai had absolutely nothing to do with Christianity before dropping into a church. This challenges our assumptions about the faith understanding of visitors. The *Emmaus* Group was very important in faith development but also the hospitality of the church was vital to the first stages of welcome; we need to be open to hospitality, welcome and exploration in our mission, including confirmation. The person happened to be from Hong Kong, but could be from England. The statistics might be quite different if there were a separate category for adults baptized from a completely non-Christian background. The ecumenical confirmation is used in Local Ecumenical Partnerships and was produced by Joint Liturgical Group.[38]

The potential for people to raise questions about their lives and about faith, particularly in an age of constant disruption, should be borne in mind.[39] The range of pastoral encounters that a church may have are usually significant potentially opening the gentle promotion of opportunities to explore the faith, as seen by Bishop Steven Croft's *Come and See* initiative[40] and the Diocese of Birmingham's *Everyday Faith* programme. [41]

Questions

- How might people learn about faith in your context?
- To what extent do you think discipleship may be caught before it is taught?
- Who might people talk to about matters of faith in your parish/ benefice?

6 Confirmation After Catechesis

Older people in a congregation will probably have received preparation for confirmation in the form of the catechism (more modern approaches to this might be Steven Croft's *Come and See*).[42] It is required in the *Book of Common Prayer* that the catechism, a question-and-answer form of learning, be memorized and that the bishop, in theory, could question the candidates at their confirmation. The catechism covered the Lord's Prayer, the Ten Commandments, the Apostles' Creed, and a section on baptism and Holy Communion. Canon B27 requires ministers who have the cure of souls to 'diligently seek out children and other persons' for confirmation after 'instruction in the Christian faith' (now we would also include preparation for receiving Communion). While there was an attempt to revise the catechism in 1990, other educational approaches have virtually completely replaced the catechism.[43]

Other methods included the confirmation class. Here a number of topics were discussed in Bible studies, or a book might be followed such as *Faith Confirmed*.[44] These classes were often a term long (10 weeks or so), covering the basics of the gospel and something about the sacraments. For many lay people this was the only teaching about sacraments that they had in their Christian life, suggesting that more preaching and study groups on the sacraments are needed. There was a tension between those who wanted to teach things to candidates and those who wanted more of a discussion. As in the wider world there was a move from conveying information to developing understanding. There was a desire to move from banking information to Christian formation. Too many people in the past (and sometimes present) had been given information, but not acted on it in the sense of becoming a regular communicant. While many were confirmed, few took this through to regular reception of Holy Communion.

Phillip remembers as a curate the *Quest* approach to confirmation where a large number of adolescents (20–30 a year) effectively formed a youth group which over two years would have some Christian teaching and activities. This would gradually lead to confirmation and many of the candidates joined the servers or the choir.

Carol-Anne

I was part of a large group of friends when we were 16, and we all attended the classes and the Friday night youth group together; it was great fun. As there were about 60 of us getting confirmed we were divided up and put into different classes, I was very shy at the time and was horrified to find that none of my friends were in the same group. Looking back, I realize that God had a very cunning plan; by me being alone in the group I was able to ask questions and share with the group in a way that I wouldn't have felt as free to do had my 'cool' friends been there.

The older minister made classes really interesting (for me) by using timelines and describing in detail what it was like to live in biblical times and the reasons why people believed and behaved the way they did and why it was different from the times we were living in. I can't remember all the details of what I learnt in class, but my picture of God grew, and I can remember really looking forward to learning more.

During our classes we were obviously told about the process we were going through, the means of grace, symbolism and so on, but I did not remember any of it until years later when I went on and later led on *Alpha* and *Emmaus*.

The big change was in the development of *Alpha*. This began in 1977 and was particularly strong across the country in the 1990s. It was more media based and allows for some discussion. There is a charismatic emphasis but no teaching on baptism and confirmation. Other courses were developed like *Emmaus* and *Pilgrim* to give a wider approach to the Christian life.

The shift in confirmation away from being an adolescent rite to that of being an adult choice questions much of the educational theory being used in such courses. Peter Ball, a canon of St Paul's, was one critic.[45] Coming from a catechumenate perspective, he argued for the whole Christian community to be a part of preparation through accompaniers, givers of hospitality, educators and an incorporation of the candidates in the life of the community. Common Worship included possible material in the Rites on the Way which are not very well known or used.[46] One criticism of the confirmation class is that an anonymous (to the congregation) group was formed and then after some time started receiving Communion. The congregation did not know who they were, so did not pray for them and were not at their confirmation (possibly done elsewhere). This led to the idea that baptism and confirmation were the work of the vicar and nothing to do with congregational life. Those who espoused a more catechumenal approach viewed the church as a 'baptizing community.'[47]

The admission of children to Communion before confirmation also had preparation opportunities. The Guidelines in GS Misc 488 said:

> Before a person is first brought to Holy Communion, the significance of the occasion should be explained to him / her and to his / her parents, and marked in some suitable way before the whole congregation…the incumbent should take care regarding the quality of teaching material, especially that used with children and young people. The material should be reviewed regularly, and the advice of diocesan officers and other professional advisers taken into account.[48]

Various materials are available to help in preparation for Communion. This does, however, complicate later confirmation preparation, as a group may now include people who have already been admitted to Communion, and those who have not. Taking confirmation classes and adapting or creating material is a key work for Christian ministers, lay and ordained, and some training in group work and adult education is a key part of training and ongoing development. In 1984 Anton Baumohl wrote the seminal book *Making Adult Disciples*, which introduced the church to adult education, and this has been further developed more recently by David Heywood in *Kingdom Learning*.[49] Both books are interested in formation of Christians and the principles in the books are entirely applicable to formation for confirmation.

Common Worship: Christian Initiation envisages seasonal patterns of initiation (pp 325 onward and particularly p 330ff). Here Easter (or Epiphany or All Saints) are points in the year where baptism and confirmation could be a key part of the life of the community. Christian initiation integrates various services into the journey of faith expressed in baptism—confirmation. Alongside these rites the assumption is that preparation is happening in some sort of group. This would need adapting for smaller churches, where this might not be an every-year event, but the principles of integrating the candidates with the community in various rites and the use of the gifts of the whole congregation (providing a venue, making cakes, being a prayer friend) could still be employed. So preparation is not just about a syllabus but also an ecclesiological approach.

Questions

- How might confirmation be owned by the whole church?
- In your church's leadership team, where does confirmation fit in your thinking?
- In an age where people sit light to commitment, what other aspects of confirmation might also be explored?

Closing Thoughts on Confirmation 7

The stories have shown that for many people confirmation is a significant step in faith. Its function for candidates, family and church has changed and continues to change—to strengthen what has occurred, to affirmation of what my family did for me as an infant, as a rite of passage (for adolescents to communicant status, now only occurring in boarding schools and large youth groups), as a staging point on my journey of faith, as a moment of review reflection and recommitment, as a recognition of my identity as a child of God.

We have seen that confirmation has three dimensions. These can be considered from a candidate-centred perspective, but I think there is also a church dimension both locally and wider. The dimensions are:

- *Pastoral*. As a step in faith of candidates and an expression of care for the nurture of Christians by the congregation.
- *Missional*. As a confession that Jesus is Lord and a time for hospitality by the congregation for family and friends and a witness to them (which can bear fruit).
- *Sacramental*.[50] An invocation of the Holy Spirit on the candidate, and a renewal of baptismal vows and acknowledgment of dependence on the Spirit by the congregation.

For those baptized as infants, confirmation is the important step of taking on the commitment made by godparents. For those baptized as adults, it is best administered at the same time as the baptism (and suitable provision needs to be made for this). For those baptized and admitted to Communion it can be seen as a rite for the affirmation of commitment to mission.

Confirmation also is an important part of the ministry of the bishop. It brings the bishop to the parish, meeting new Christians and those stepping forward in faith, meeting the local Christian community.

The main role of the confirmation service can be seen as the giving of a gift from a generous God who loves his children. There is no limit to God's generosity and that is so freely given in confirmation and the gift of the Holy Spirit—the sevenfold gifts of the Spirit. That sense of God believing in us and coming to us, confirming us in faith and for faith.[51]

Bishops have varied in how they do this, but most are diligent in their duty.

Confirmation has for a long time been linked to catechesis. The latter by the changes in educational theory has changed from something by rote to discussion and learning. It is an opportunity for the congregation to become a learning church and it is important that many are involved in the process, not only in leading discussion, but in hosting, providing cake and in intercession. Rites on the Way suggest a number of possible ways of incorporation of the people of God in the process. We need to move on from the distanced confirmation class and enable confirmation to be owned by the whole congregation.

In an age of identity politics, we need to remember our Christian identity. To quote the catechism, 'In my baptism…I was made…the child of God.' Perhaps this never fully sinks in but confirmation it a time to affirm and celebrate this fact. It helps shape us in all we do the more we meditate on it. It also includes a freedom to become what you are, which is an exploration with the Holy Spirit. Confirmation can be a part of that process.

As the stories show, how people come to faith is very varied. Confirmation is a part of the Anglican treasure house. It has evolved but still speaks. As a child of God, we have access to God's riches heaped up for us, as Robert Louis Stevenson says:

> All of us had an ample share of the treasure, and used it wisely or foolishly, according to our natures.[52]

Notes

1 P Tovey, *Of Water and the Spirit: Mission and the Baptismal Liturgy* (London: Canterbury Press, 2015).
2 P Tovey, *Anglican Baptismal Liturgies* (London: Canterbury Press, 2017).
3 I refer here to the theories of Puller and Mason.
4 P Tovey, *Anglican Confirmation 1662–1820* (Aldershot: Ashgate, 2014).
5 Data supplied by the Data Services Team at the National Church Institutions.
6 F Knight, *The Nineteenth-century Church and English Society* (Cambridge University Press, 2010).
7 See https://www.elizabethi.org/contents/earlyyears/christening.htm
8 F Procter and W Frere, *A New History of the Book of Common Prayer with a Rationale of Its Offices* (London: Macmillan, 1958) p 606.
9 M Perry, *Crisis for Confirmation* (London: SCM, 1967).
10 M Ramsey, *Durham Essays and Addresses* (London: SPCK, 1957).
11 P Tovey, *Eighteenth-century Anglican Confirmation*, JLS 79 (Norwich: Ancient and Modern, 2015).
12 For the present position see *Confirmation FAQs*: https://www.churchofengland.org/life-events/confirmations/confirmation-faqs#na
13 The Archbishops' Commission on Christian Doctrine, *Christian Initiation: Birth and Growth in a Christian Society*, GS 30 (Cowley: Church Army Press, p 42).
14 *ibid*, p 15.
15 *ibid*, p 18.
16 The Church of England Education Office, *Rooted in the Church* (2016) https://www.churchofengland.org/sites/default/files/2017-10/2016_rooted_in_the_church_summary_report.pdf p 3.
17 *ibid*, p 32.
18 *Eg* the Diocese of Guildford, 'Christian Initiation and the Admission of Children to Holy Communion before Confirmation': https://www.cofeguildford.org.uk/about/governance/diocesan-procedures-policies-and-regulations/public-worship/christian-initiation-and-the-admission-of-children-to-holy-communion-before-confirmation
19 https://www.churchofengland.org/about/leadership-and-governance/legal-services/canons-church-england/section-b
20 'Admission of the Baptized to Communion,' *Common Worship: Baptism and Confirmation Services* (London: Church House Publishing, 2022) pp 156–160.
21 The Church in Wales, *Children and Holy Communion* (2002): https://churchinwales.contentfiles.net/media/documents/Children_and_Holy_Communion.pdf
22 Commission, *Patterns for Baptism* (London: Church House Publishing, 2022) p 107.
23 See M Thurian, *Consecration of the Layman: New Approaches to the Sacrament of Confirmation* (Baltimore, MD: Helicon, 1963).
24 Affirmation of Baptismal Faith, *Common Worship: Baptism and Confirmation Services* (London: Church House Publishing, 2022) pp 384–408.
25 Resource Material for the Beginning of a New Year, *Common Worship: Times and Seasons* (London: Church House Publishing, 2006) pp 105–115.
26 Anglican Church of Kenya, *Our Modern Services* (Nairobi: Uzima Press, 2002) pp 57–63.
27 Small Working Group, *A Recommended Revision of the Liturgy for Baptism and Replacement of the Liturgy for the Laying on of Hands for Confirmation and Renewal* (2016). For a discussion of this see Bosco Peters, *The End of Confirmation?*

https://liturgy.co.nz/the-end-of-confirmation The original documents appear to have been removed from the internet.

28 Church of England, *Statistics for Mission 2019*, https://www.churchofengland.org/sites/default/files/2020-10/2019StatisticsForMission.pdf, p 9.

29 For baptism those over 10 are categorized in the adult group. For confirmation the adult is taken as over 20 years old.

30 F Bennett, 'Indiscriminate Confirmation,' *Theology*, 1945, pp 73–77.

31 p x.

32 See https://www.youtube.com/watch?v=C_tOiQOG_g4

33 See D R Holeton, *Growing in Newness of Life* (Toronto: Anglican Book Centre, 1993) p 229.

34 Roman Catholic Church, *The Code of Canon Law* (Bangalore: Collins, 1983, 2001) p 163.

35 The report can be found at https://www.bwanet.org/old-site/images/pdf/baptist-anglican-dialogue.pdf

36 Church of England, *Common Worship Christian Initiation* (London: Church House Publishing, 2006) p 197 ff.

37 *ibid*, p 211 ff.

38 See P Tovey, *Anglican Baptismal Liturgies* (Norwich: Canterbury Press, 2017) Appendix C, p 311.

39 See H Thompson, *Disorder: Hard Times in the 21st Century* (Oxford University Press, 2022) for an historical assessment of the recent past and the times we are now living through pertaining to disorder.

40 https://www.oxford.anglican.org/campaigns/come-and-see/come-and-see.php

41 https://www.cofebirmingham.com/everyday-faith/

42 https://www.oxford.anglican.org/come-and-see/

43 Church of England, *A New Revised Catechism* (London: CIO, 1990, 1996).

44 J Stott, *Your Confirmation* (London: Hodder, 1973). G Reid, *To be Confirmed* (London: Hodder, 1977). H Montefiore, *Confirmation Notebook* (London: SPCK, 1986). There have been many books written for those being confirmed which can be used a study books.

45 P Ball, *Adult Believing* (London: Mowbray, 1988). P Ball and M Grundy, *Faith on the Way* (London: Continuum, 2000).

46 Church of England, *Common Worship: Christian Initiation* (London: Church House Publishing, 2006) p 15 ff. All this material is 'commended' and so can be adapted as locally necessary.

47 A T Eastman, *The Baptizing Community* (New York: Seabury Press, 1985)

48 D Murrie and J Hall, *Children and Communion: A Review* (GS1576, 2005).

49 A Baumohl, *Making Adult Disciples* (London: Scripture Union, 1984). D Heywood, *Kingdom Learning* (London: SCM, 2017).

50 While not a sacrament and arguable a pastoral rite we use the term 'sacramental' in the secondary nature it implies while not diminishing the experience of the Spirit in any way.

51 Bishop Mark Davies in P Maidment, S Mapledoram with S Lake, *Reconnecting with Confirmation* (London: Church House Publishing, 2011) p 135

52 R L Stevenson, *Treasure Island* (London: The Folio Society, 1963, originally published by London: Cassell & Company, 1883) p 222.